An *Extreme* Dive *Under the* Antarctic Ice

Brad Matsen

Enslow Publishers, Inc.

40 Industrial Road   PO Box 38
Box 398   Aldershot
Berkeley Heights, NJ 07922   Hants GU12 6BP
USA   UK
http://www.enslow.com

Library of Congress Cataloging-in-Publication Data

Matsen, Bradford.
   An extreme dive under the Antarctic ice / Brad Matsen.
      v. cm. — (Incredible deep-sea adventures)
   Includes bibliographical references and index.
   Contents: On the Antarctic Ice—The Mission Beneath the Ice—Into the Freezing
Ocean—Descent to the Bottom—Back to the Surface.
   ISBN 0-7660-2190-4 (hardcover)
   1. Deep diving—Antarctica—Ross Sea—Juvenile literature. 2. Underwater
exploration—Antarctica—Ross Sea—Juvenile literature. [1. Deep diving—Antarctica—
Ross Sea. 2. Underwater exploration—Antarctica—Ross Sea.] I. Title.
   GC65.M366 2003
   551.46'07'091674—dc21
                                                                2002155040

Printed in the United States of America

10 9 8 7 6 5 4 3 2 1

To Our Readers: We have done our best to make sure all Internet Addresses in this book
were active and appropriate when we went to press. However, the author and the
publisher have no control over and assume no liability for the material available on those
Internet sites or on other Web sites they may link to. Any comments or suggestions can
be sent by e-mail to comments@enslow.com or to the address on the back cover.

Photo Credits: © 1999 Artville, LLC, p. 17 (map); Lynn Teo Simarski, National
Science Foundation, p. 15; Photo by Pat Iampietro, pp. 4, 5, 6, 8, 9, 11, 12, 13, 14, 17
(photos), 19, 20, 22, 23, 25, 29, 38, 39, 40–41, 42–43; NOAA, pp. 21, 27; National
Science Foundation, pp. 1, 30, 44–48; © 2003 Norbert Wu, www.norbertwu.com, pp.
3, 32, 34, 36.

Cover Photos: Photo by Pat Iampietro (diver, penguin); National Science Foundation
(seal).

Contents

CHAPTER 1

On
the *Antarctic*
Ice

Scientist Pat Iampietro (Yaam-pee-ET-row) is very excited. He is on his way to his first dive under Antarctic ice. He rides in a snow Spryte with two other divers. This truck has rubber-and-steel tracks instead of wheels. It is like a bulldozer with a passenger cabin. The tracks rattle and clank over the ice and snow.

Inside the snow Spryte, the noise of the engine and tracks is very loud. Outside, the wind is howling. The temperature is −30 degrees Fahrenheit (−34 degrees Celsius). The air is full of blowing snow and ice crystals. It is a typical day in Antarctica.

Pat Iampietro is a scientist who studies the ocean. He is also an experienced diver. He has been underwater in many places around the world, but this will be his first dive under the Antarctic ice.

"It's really like going into outer space," Iampietro said. "I couldn't wait."[1]

A World of Ice

Antarctica is the coldest continent on Earth. Temperatures fall to –76 degrees Fahrenheit (–60 degrees Celsius) in the winter. The coldest temperature ever recorded on Earth was –128.6 degrees Fahrenheit (–89.2 degrees Celsius). This was recorded at the Russian research station on July 21, 1983.[2]

ANTARCTICA IS A COLD BUT BEAUTIFUL CONTINENT.

Most of Antarctica is covered with ice all year. Underneath the ice it is rock. Antarctica is surrounded by water. The ocean around the continent freezes, too. In the winter, the sea ice completely surrounds Antarctica.

More than 90 percent of the ice in the world is in Antarctica! The ice on land is three miles thick in some places. If the ice of Antarctica melted, the earth's oceans would rise 200 feet (60 meters)![3]

Getting to Antarctica

In the noisy snow Spryte, Iampietro and the other scientists have to yell to talk to each other. They talk about their long and harrowing trip to Antarctica. They almost didn't get there at all.

First they flew on an airliner from Los Angeles to Auckland, New Zealand. That took twelve hours. Then they flew to Christchurch in southern New Zealand. That took another two hours.

In Christchurch, they received extreme weather equipment at the Antarctica staging base. They got heavy socks, gloves, and down parkas. Without this special gear, they could not survive in Antarctica.

The scientists also received training for living in the extreme climate of Antarctica from experts at the staging base. They were told to always keep their bare skin covered. Otherwise it would freeze solid. They were also told to drink lots of water. Antarctica is the driest place on Earth. Without

lots of water, a person can become dehydrated. This can lead to exhaustion and sickness.

Finally they boarded a Hercules C-130 plane to take them to McMurdo Station, Antarctica. The flight was supposed to take eight hours. The big four-engine plane roared off the runway and into clear skies over New Zealand.

On they flew. The ride was rough. The C-130 is a military transport plane. The seats are not very comfortable. The noise of the engines is very loud. There are no movies or flight attendants.

They had been in the air for four hours when the pilot made an announcement. They were halfway to Antarctica, but the weather at McMurdo Station was too bad to land. They were turning back to Christchurch! The C-130 made a U-turn in the sky and flew four hours back to New Zealand.

The next day they took off again. Once more, they flew four hours toward Antarctica. Then came the dreaded announcement from the pilot. The wind was too high for a landing at McMurdo Station. Everyone on the plane groaned. Would they ever get to Antarctica?

On the third try they made it. Everyone cheered when the plane flew past the halfway mark. Four hours later they saw McMurdo Station out the windows. The camp was just some low buildings near the runway. Ice and snow were everywhere. It looked cold and rugged. But it was a welcome sight.[4]

The scientists rested for two days at McMurdo Station. Then they were on their way to dive under the ice.

AFTER SEVERAL LONG DAYS, THE SCIENTISTS FINALLY SPOT ANTARCTICA FROM THE WINDOW OF THEIR PLANE.

The Dangers of Ice Diving

The snow Spryte rattles and clanks. The wind howls. Pat Iampietro thinks about the dive he is about to make.

Before Iampietro was cleared to dive under the ice, a diving safety officer at McMurdo Station checked him out. The safety officer inspected all his equipment. Iampietro will wear a thick rubber diving suit to keep out the cold water. He will put on long wool underwear under his diving suit and two pairs of wool socks.

Iampietro will wear swim fins, a face mask, and a belt with lead weights on it. The weights will help him sink to the bottom. He will have a scuba tank of air on his back. He will breathe through a hose from the tank. The hose is connected to the tank through a valve called a regulator. The regulator is a special kind for diving in cold water.

The cold water is very dangerous for two reasons. First, if the regulator freezes, the air in the tank will drain in a minute or two. Then the diver will have no more air to breathe. Second, if the valve on the hose that inflates a diver's suit freezes, air will flow freely into the suit. When this happens, the suit blows up like a balloon. The diver's swim fins pop off. His weight belt pops off. The diver shoots to the surface. But he hits the ice instead of open water. He gets pinned underneath the ice.

The safety officer told Iampietro to be sure he knows where the hole in the ice is at all times. Finding direction is not always easy. Compasses do not work well in Antarctica. The magnetism of the nearby South Pole throws them off. Divers have to navigate using landmarks on the bottom of the ocean. And they always try to keep the diving hole or its rope in sight. It is hard to estimate distances under the ice, though. In the clear water, things look closer than they really are.[5]

The Hole in the Ice

After two hours, the engine of the snow Spryte slows down. Pat Iampietro and the other scientists have reached the hut that is set up over the hole in the ice where

THE DIVE HOLE IS DRILLED WITH AN ICE AUGER ATTACHED TO A SNOW SPRYTE. WHEN THE HOLE IS READY, A DIVE HUT WILL BE SET UP AROUND IT.

SLUSH ICE MUST BE CLEARED FROM THE DIVE HOLE.

they will dive. They unload their equipment and take it into the hut.

A support crew set up the dive hut a few days earlier. They also drilled the hole through the ice for the divers with an ice auger. An ice auger is a huge screw mounted on a snow Spryte. It is powered by an engine. The ice is eight feet thick, but the auger is powerful enough to drill through it. The dive hole is 4 feet (1.2 meters) wide. The support crew covered it with a trapdoor.

The dive hut is the size of a small garage. It protects the divers from the howling wind. Kerosene heaters keep the

A SNOW SPRYTE IS USED TO DRAG THE DIVE HUT OUT TO THE HOLE IN THE ICE.

dive hut warm. The hut has benches where the scientists can rest between dives. They bring snacks, soup, and coffee with them. Each diver can make up to three or four dives in one day. They return to McMurdo Station to sleep.

The dive hut sometimes has a shelf of computers and video players. The divers can then preview the videotapes they take on the bottom. They can look them over in the dive hut to be sure they are getting results. Then they bring their samples and tapes to their lab at McMurdo Station.[6]

It is time for the divers to put on their equipment. They are ready to dive under the Antarctic ice.

CHAPTER 2

The
Mission Beneath
the Ice

Diving under the ice is exciting. But Pat Iampietro and the other scientists are in Antarctica to do a job. What are they looking for? Why do they dive under the ice?

The answer lies at McMurdo Station. About 1,200 scientists and support crew live there during the Antarctic summer, from October to February. During the winter, from March to September, about 200 people live at McMurdo Station.[1]

McMurdo Station is the largest base in Antarctica. It was started by the U.S. Navy in 1956. There are forty other research stations in Antarctica. Many nations send scientists to Antarctica.[2]

MCMURDO STATION, OTHERWISE KNOWN AS MACTOWN, HAS EVERYTHING FROM A LOCAL NEWSPAPER TO BOWLING ALLEYS.

Scientists at McMurdo Station live in two- and three-story dormitories. Two people share each room. They cook and eat in another building. For entertainment, they have a bowling alley, science lectures, and dances.[3]

McMurdo Station is like a small town. The people living there produce a lot of garbage and waste. Most of it is shipped back to the United States and recycled. But some goes into a dump on the ice and then into the sea. Wastewater from bathrooms and kitchens goes into the sea, too. Pat Iampietro and his team are diving under the ice to see how this garbage and waste is affecting life in Antarctica's surrounding oceans.

The Mission

The scientists' mission is to study the pollution at the bottom of the ocean. The divers will use special tools called core samplers to take samples of sediment from the bottom. They will analyze the samples in their lab. They will be able to tell if oil, chemicals, or other pollutants are in the sediment.

The divers carry video cameras that they call "data guns." They will analyze what they see on videotape back in the lab. They are looking for evidence of pollution, such as garbage and wrecked equipment on the bottom. They will also capture fish, clams, and other creatures. The health of the animals will tell them whether pollution in the water and sediment is causing the animals harm.[4]

McMurdo Station is 15 miles (24 kilometers) away from the dive hole. Pollution from the station has reached that far out into the ocean. Although the scientific research going on in Antarctica is important, Pat Iampietro and other scientists are worried about the damage the researchers and tourists are causing in the sea around McMurdo Station. The environment of Antarctica is precious and fragile.

The Great White Continent

Antarctica is the fifth largest continent on Earth. It covers 5.4 million square miles (14 million square kilometers). That is almost one and a half times the size of the United States, or twice as big as Australia. Antarctica is surrounded by the southern reaches of the Indian, Atlantic,

THE WILDERNESS OF THE ANTARCTIC IS SLOWLY BEING POLLUTED. MANY PEOPLE ARE NOW WORKING TO FIX THIS PROBLEM.

and Pacific Oceans (an area sometimes called the Antarctic Ocean). It is the stormiest sea on Earth.

Antarctica is also the driest place on Earth. Only 1.5 to 3 inches (3.8 to 7.6 centimeters) of moisture falls each year. That is less than the moisture that falls in deserts. Most of the moisture is snow. Very little of the snow ever melts. It builds up and is compressed into ice over thousands of years.[5]

Antarctica is the windiest place on Earth. The center of the continent is much higher than the coastline. Wind flows down from the center to the coast. This is called katabatic gravity wind. Great storms and blizzards bring winds of over 100 miles (160 kilometers) per hour.[6]

Mostly scientists, explorers, and support crews live in Antarctica. (Only Argentina and Chile have bases where families live.) The scientists are there because Antarctica is so interesting and different from other places on Earth. It is a perfect laboratory for studying extreme conditions.

A treaty was signed in 1998 by all twenty-seven nations with bases in Antarctica. They agreed to clean up the waste and pollution they had caused around their bases. They also agreed to reduce the amount of waste and pollution in the future.[7]

"Antarctica should be preserved simply because it represents for us all a place of pristine whiteness," said environmentalist John May. "In an increasingly polluted world, this clean and largely unspoiled area should [not] be lost."[8]

Suiting Up for a Dive

Pat Iampietro and the other divers unpack their equipment. They help each other put on diving suits. They close their suits with big zippers. The suits have tight

THE WILDERNESS OF THE ANTARCTIC IS SLOWLY BEING POLLUTED. MANY PEOPLE ARE NOW WORKING TO FIX THIS PROBLEM.

rubber around the wrists and neck. Freezing water in a diving suit can be extremely dangerous.

The ice divers carefully attach regulators to their air tanks. They turn the valves on the top of their air tanks and the air flows through a hose to their mouthpieces. They test their breathing mouthpieces. They check their masks, fins, and weight belts. They check each other's equipment just to be sure. Safety is the number one concern for divers.

It is not safe to get in the water until divers carefully check all of their equipment.

After days of flying and hours in a snow Spryte, they are ready to dive. Now, Pat Iampietro and the other two divers open the trapdoor. The hole is full of ice chips. The water looks like slush. Iampietro shivers. He is about to make his first dive under the ice in Antarctica.

CHAPTER 3

Into the *Freezing* Ocean

**P**at Iampietro is going into the water first. He sits on the ice at the edge of the hole. He looks one last time at the other two divers who will follow him. The divers make an "O" shape with their thumb and fingers. This is the divers' sign that everything is OK.

The time has come. Iampietro plunges feetfirst into the icy water. "The cold hit me right away," he said. "The exposed skin between my suit and diving mask was freezing."[1]

The ice is 8 feet (2.4 meters) thick. Iampietro has jumped into a tunnel of freezing cold water. He rests on the surface to catch his breath. Then he descends

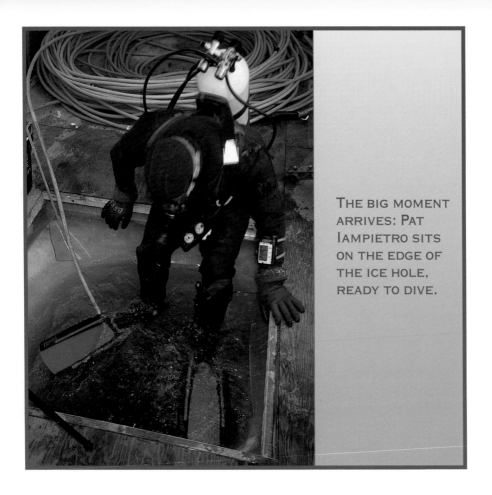

THE BIG MOMENT ARRIVES: PAT IAMPIETRO SITS ON THE EDGE OF THE ICE HOLE, READY TO DIVE.

out of the ice tunnel. Now the ice is a solid ceiling of white above him. The ice shimmers with the light of the sun.

A rope hangs from the diving hole. The rope has black-and-white checkered flags on it. They make the rope easier to see. A winking strobe light marks the bottom of the rope. A few hundred yards away is another rope leading to a safety hole. If a diver loses track of the main hole, he can swim to the safety hole.

Crystal Clear Water

Iampietro is startled by how clear the water is. Usually a diver can see only a few feet underwater. Under the Antarctic ice, though, he can see 600 feet (180 meters). Even though he is already cold, he is thrilled. "It was amazingly clear, kind of dark, but clearer than any water I'd ever been in," he said.[2]

The water under the ice is clear for two reasons. First, there are no waves, so sand and silt are not churned up from the bottom. Second, the light under the ice is dim. Tiny plants called phytoplankton that float in the water need lots of light

IAMPIETRO BOBS IN THE ICE HOLE, GETTING USED TO THE FRIGID WATER.

to grow. Because the light here is dim, there is very little phytoplankton in the water. This makes the water clearer.

Iampietro sinks down a few more feet. Scuba diving is like floating in space. A diver can control his buoyancy. This lets him hover weightlessly in the water. Iampietro hangs motionless in the water and looks around.

He sees a seal swim by in the distance. Other divers told him that seals like to swim to the holes in the ice. They told him to be careful when he is coming to the surface. Sometimes a seal will be in the diving hole. It might fight a diver for control of the hole.

So far so good. Iampietro's equipment is working well. He feels calm and confident. He continues his descent but always looks around. He sees the two other divers swim down through the hole. He will try to keep an eye on them for safety. They will watch him, too.[3]

He looks down and sees the gray mud of the bottom. It is 100 feet (30 meters) below. Soon he will be down there. Then it will be time to go to work. Scientists dive under the ice in Antarctica to do a job. For now, though, Pat descends and enjoys his dive.

The Wonders of Antarctica

Everyone who visits Antarctica is amazed by the creatures they see. Even tourists can now explore on land and dive under the ice. Scientists have jobs to do, but they also take time to just look around. The creatures in Antarctica are awesome.

EMPEROR PENGUINS ARE AN EXAMPLE OF THE AMAZING WILDLIFE FOUND IN ANTARCTICA.

Life in Antarctica is very different from any place else on Earth. The plants and animals that live there have adapted to the cold. Penguins, other birds, and rats are the only large animals that live on land in Antarctica.[4]

Penguins are flightless birds. Their wings help them swim underwater. They live on the ice but spend a lot of their time in the ocean. Pat Iampietro and other divers often see them in the water. They are fast, curious, and very good hunters.[5]

Five kinds of penguins live in Antarctica. The biggest of all are the emperor penguins. They can weigh up to 70 pounds (31.5 kilograms) and can be 3 feet (1 meter) tall. These beautiful black-and-white creatures are the world's largest diving birds. Emperor penguins can stay underwater for up to nine minutes without taking a breath. They can swim almost 1,000 feet (300 meters) deep to eat plankton and fish.[6]

Most Life Is in the Sea

Life on Antarctica's frozen land and ice is harsh and dangerous. That is why most creatures live under the ice in the sea. The water is cold but the temperature is constant.

Most animals are food for other animals. Big animals eat small animals. Some animals eat the remains of dead animals. Tiny animals called zooplankton and krill eat plants that grow in the ocean. All the animals depend on each other for survival. They are part of what is called the food web.

The Small but Mighty Krill

Krill is a Norwegian word. It means "small fry." Krill are a kind of animal called a crustacean. They are related to crabs, lobsters, and shrimp. Krill swim together in giant swarms. They eat by filtering huge amounts of water through their bodies. In that water are even tinier animals, pieces of animals, and microscopic plants.

KRILL ARE A VERY IMPORTANT SOURCE OF FOOD FOR MANY ANTARCTIC ANIMALS.

Krill are very small. The largest krill are 1½ inches (3.8 centimeters) long. Krill are the most important part of the Antarctic food web. They are a huge source of food. All the krill in the southern oceans together weigh almost a billion tons! Many other animals that live in Antarctic waters eat krill or eat other animals that eat krill.[7]

Super-cool Fish

About 20,000 different kinds of fish live in the oceans of the world. Only 120 kinds of fish live in the sea near Antarctica.[8] The fish that live there have special antifreeze chemicals. These chemicals keep ice from forming in their bodies. If they did not have this antifreeze, they would freeze solid.[9]

Most of the kinds of fish that live around Antarctica do not live in any other oceans. Ice fish are the most unusual. They are the only known fish without red blood. The blood of ice fish is clear with a yellow tint. This is because its blood does not carry many red cells. This helps them live in very cold water.[10]

Most fish in Antarctic waters live near the bottom. They feed on plants, small crabs, and other creatures of the ocean floor. They also eat some krill that settles to the mud. These bottom feeders are usually very small fish. Most are less than 6 inches (15 centimeters) long.

The Antarctic toothfish (also called Chilean sea bass) is the largest fish in Antarctic waters. It has a very light skeleton. It also has a lot of fat. Fat floats. Their lighter bodies allow toothfish to swim off the bottom. Krill are most plentiful in the middle of the water. Toothfish get more to eat and grow bigger than bottom-feeding fish. Toothfish can grow to 5 feet (1.5 meters) long.[11]

A Sea of Seals

Antarctica is paradise for seals. These marine mammals keep warm because they have blubber and fur. Seals hunt under the ice for fish, squid, and krill. They crawl up on the ice to rest. Seals have lungs, so they must come to the surface to breathe air.

Six kinds of seals live in the ocean off Antarctica. They are Ross seals, southern elephant seals, Weddell seals, crabeater seals, Antarctic fur seals, and the ferocious leopard seals.

WEDDELL SEALS RELAX ON THE ICE IN BETWEEN DIVES. IN THE PAST, THESE SEALS WERE HUNTED BY EXPLORERS.

Antarctic fur seals are the smallest. They grow to 6 feet (2 meters) long. They weigh about 450 pounds (200 kilograms). Elephant seals are the giants of Antarctica. A full-grown male is 15 feet (4.6 meters) long and weighs over 8,000 pounds (3,600 kilograms)!

Leopard seals are the terrors of the Antarctic sea. Female leopard seals are 10 feet (3 meters) long and weigh 770 pounds (350 kilograms). These sleek, slender seals are very fast swimmers. Leopard seals have powerful jaws and sharp teeth. They are fierce solitary hunters. They eat krill but also attack other seals and swimming birds. Once, a leopard seal attacked a man crossing the ice.[12]

The Greatest Krill Eaters

The largest animal that ever lived feeds on krill in Antarctic waters. Blue whales grow to over 100 feet (30 meters) long. That's longer than two school buses. They weigh 200 tons or more. That's more than one hundred cars.

Blue whales gulp water full of krill. Then they push the water through filters in their mouths called baleen. Most of the water goes back into the sea. The whale swallows the krill. That's a meal.

TODAY SEALS IN THE ANTARCTIC ARE PROTECTED FROM HUNTERS. HERE, AN ELEPHANT SEAL POSES FOR THE CAMERA.

As many as 200,000 blue whales have been known to swim to Antarctica to feed on krill. Over the years, whalers killed almost all of them. Now only 1,000 are left.[13] The Antarctic Treaty and other treaties protect blue whales and other marine mammals. Although blue whales were almost extinct, they now have a chance to survive.

Five other kinds of baleen whales feed on krill in Antarctica. They are fin whales, humpback whales, minke whales, southern right whales, and sei whales.

Other kinds of whales visit Antarctic waters, too. They are called toothed whales. They have teeth instead of baleen. They feed on squid, fish, and even seals. The toothed whales are sperm whales, orca whales, and southern bottlenose dolphins.

Whales are migratory animals. They make long journeys in the ocean. They do not stay in one place for very long. Most whales spend part of the year in warmer water. They have their young there. Then they go to Antarctica to feed on the rich krill, squid, and other animals. The whales get fat and strong in Antarctic waters. Some divers have been lucky enough to see whales.

Everyone who dives under the Antarctic ice is thrilled when they see the magnificent creatures that live there. But scientists such as Pat Iampietro also dive to continue an important mission.

CHAPTER 4

Descent to the *Bottom*

**P**at Iampietro is in the ocean under the ice. He checks his depth gauge. It tells him he is 100 feet (30 meters) from the surface. The bottom is coming up quickly. He double checks his equipment. The regulator is still working fine. He checks his watch. He has been in the water for ten minutes.

Iampietro is very cold. He cannot feel the skin around his face mask. His hands and feet are freezing. He knows he has to be very careful. Iampietro looks up at the ice.

He had turned away from the ice hole as he descended. For a minute he can't find it. Then he sees the winking strobe light on the bottom of the rope.

He spots the rope with the black-and-white flags. His eyes follow it up. Check. He knows where the hole is. Then he looks around and finds the safety hole. Check.

Iampietro adjusts the air in his diving suit. This slows down his descent. He hovers just above the bottom. He checks his core sampler and video camera. He is ready to go to work.

Amazing Life on the Bottom

"It's really amazing down there on the bottom," said Pat Iampietro. "There are giant worms and sponges that are nowhere else in the world. And there are so many different kinds of critters."[1]

The bottom of the ocean around Antarctica is a lively place. Millions of animals make their home there, though many are very small and you have to know where to look for them. The bottom is made of gray and black mud, cinders, and rocks.

Sea stars are everywhere. Iampietro says the bottom of the ocean off Antarctica looks like a galaxy.[2] Many animals are splashes of color against the dark bottom. Bright sponges, corals, and sea anemones decorate the rocks.

The animals that live on the bottom off Antarctica grow very slowly. This is because the water is so cold. Food is hard to find. Everything slows down.

Many of the Antarctic bottom animals are larger and live much longer than their relatives in warmer waters. Scientists think this is because they grow more slowly in the cold water

THE ANTARCTIC FLOOR IS FULL OF LIFE, INCLUDING BRIGHT RED SEA STARS.

and therefore do not use as much energy. Some sponges grow to be giants more than three feet (one meter) across. That is many times bigger than most warm-water sponges. Some Antarctic sponges live for several centuries.[3]

Burrowing into the mud is a good way to survive in Antarctic waters, too. Clams dig in and eat food that drifts by. Worms, too, live in the mud. One giant worm can reach six feet (two meters) in length.[4] Divers call them rainbow worms because of their bright colors. They also call them slime worms because they are so slimy.[5]

Pat Iampietro is amazed at what he sees on his first dive and others that follow. He watches seals and penguins swimming. He looks up and sees the shimmering ceiling of ice. He looks down and sees the galaxy of animals on the bottom coming toward him.

"There were so many beautiful animals. It was hard to keep my mind on my work," said Pat Iampietro. "I felt very lucky to be there."[6]

Getting the Job Done

Iampietro settles on his knees on the bottom. He checks his watch. He knows he is so fascinated by what he sees that he might lose track of time. He has to begin his trip to the surface in just five minutes.

Then he takes another look around. The light is dim at 100 feet but he can see pretty well. He is kneeling on hard-packed mud. He sees clam holes in the mud. He sees worm tracks. He sees the tubes of other worms that burrow in the mud.

There are some rocks off to his right. They are covered with small sponges. He sees a very large sponge just beyond the rocks. He also sees sea urchins on the rocks. They are reddish brown with sharp spines. He sees an ice fish swim by. Then another. Then, wow, there's a giant rainbow worm. It is about three feet (one meter) long.

A SEA STAR IN THE WATERS OF ANTARCTICA CLIMBS UP THE STALK OF A FANWORM. THE WORM LIVES IN A TUBE AND HAS FEATHERY GILLS TO GATHER FOOD PARTICLES FROM THE WATER.

"You have to be a naturalist," he said. "You want to look around and remember what you see." Iampietro makes a videotape to study the scene again back in his lab.[7]

Then he takes some core samples. The sampling tools look like coffee cans. He presses one down into the mud. Then he pulls the sampler out. It is now filled with a plug of sediment from the ocean bottom. He covers the open end of the sampler with a plastic top and slips the sampler into its carrying case. Then he takes two more cores.

He only has time to pick up a few clams. They are lying on the mud near where he took the core samples. The mud and the clams will tell how bad the pollution is on the bottom. Iampietro takes one last look around. He checks his watch. He makes sure his samples are secure. It is time to start for the surface.

CHAPTER 5

Back to
the
Surface

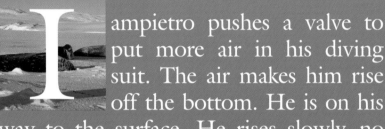ampietro pushes a valve to put more air in his diving suit. The air makes him rise off the bottom. He is on his way to the surface. He rises slowly, no faster than the bubbles of air coming from his regulator. This is to prevent sickness from gas bubbles in his body.

He kicks his fins as he goes up, swimming toward the rope. He adjusts the air in his diving suit to make sure he doesn't rise too fast. He looks down and sees the other two divers starting for the surface, too. He will be the first one to the hole.

He reaches the rope with the black-and-white flags. Now he can go straight up. He plans to stop his ascent

DANGER! A LEOPARD SEAL IS SWIMMING IN IAMPIETRO'S DIVE HOLE. THESE SEALS ARE FIERCE HUNTERS WITH SHARP TEETH.

for a few minutes to rest. That will let his body gases adjust to the surface. His first dive under Antarctic ice is almost over. Iampietro looks up at the hole. Leopard seal![1]

A Seal in the Ice Hole

The seal is about 15 feet (4.6 meters) above Iampietro at the mouth of the ice tunnel. It is thrashing around in the hole. Iampietro is excited at first. He is glad to see the beautiful animal. Then he gets a little scared. He has read about leopard seals and knows they can be very dangerous.

He thinks of waiting for the other divers. But he is very cold and his air is running low. Iampietro waves one of his arms. This just seems to make the seal curious about him. Then the seal leaves the hole and swims down! It makes a close pass at Iampietro, who is hanging on to the rope.

Iampietro has seen seals on other dives in warm water. The leopard seal just looks mean, though. Iampietro hangs on to the rope and watches the sleek, beautiful seal. The seal is incredibly fast. It turns with blinding speed. Then the seal loses interest. Maybe the big creature in a black suit hanging from a rope does not look enough like a meal. The seal swims away in the cold Antarctic sea.

THE DIVERS REST IN THE HUT BEFORE HEADING UNDER THE ICE AGAIN.

Back in the Warm Dive Hut

Iampietro swims up through the tunnel where the seal had been. He bobs to the surface of the ice hole. First he hands the support crew his samples and video camera. He passes up his tank, weight belt, and mask. Then he hauls himself out onto the floor of the hut like a seal.

The warmth of the hut feels great. The other divers surface in the hole. In the dive hut, they slap him on the back. Pat Iampietro has made his first dive under Antarctic ice. The

divers keep their suits on but rest for an hour. They eat some soup and sandwiches. They store the core samples in bags. It is just another day of work under the ice.

Iampietro looks at his first videotape of the bottom. He had been nervous and excited. But the tape is fine. It shows the rocks, the sponges, and the clam holes. He has done his job.

Pat Iampietro is now officially an Antarctic ice diver.

"It was wonderful," he said. "And it just kept getting better with every dive."[2]

SCIENTISTS AND OTHER RESEARCHERS WANT TO MAKE SURE THAT HUMANS DO NOT SPOIL THE PRISTINE ENVIRONMENT OF ANTARCTICA.

Pat Iampietro and his team stayed in Antarctica for three more weeks. They made about fifty dives each under the ice. Then they went back to their home base in Monterey, California.

They compare the results of their work with results from earlier expeditions. Scientists have been studying the pollution

from McMurdo Station since 1992. Everyone knows people are damaging the environment around the station, but their work helps show exactly what is happening beneath the ice.

In January 2003, a new system for cleaning wastewater started running. The treatment removes solid materials before wastewater is sent into the sea. This is the same kind of system used in many cities. Iampietro and other scientists will return to Antarctica to see how the system is working.

Pat Iampietro knows that the work he and other scientists do under the ice helps to preserve the balance between humans and nature in Antarctica. He hopes that he will return in twenty years and find that the creatures in the sea around the Great White Continent are even healthier than they were on his very first dive. He also hopes that sharing his experience will inspire others to study the ocean and maybe make an incredible dive under the Antarctic ice themselves.[3]

Chapter Notes

CHAPTER 1. ON THE ANTARCTIC ICE

1. Author interview with Pat Iampietro, October 24, 2002.
2. Sanford Moss, *Natural History of the Antarctic Peninsula* (New York: Columbia University Press, 1988), pp. 13–17.
3. John May, *The Greenpeace Book of Antarctica* (London: Dorling Kindersley Limited, 1989), p. 20.
4. Iampietro interview.
5. Ibid.
6. Ibid.

CHAPTER 2. THE MISSION BENEATH THE ICE

1. U.S. Central Intelligence Agency, *The World Factbook, 2002,* "Antarctica" © 2002, <http://www.odci.gov/cia/publications/factbook/geos/ay.htm> (November 10, 2002).
2. Marilyn J. Landis, *Antarctica: Exploring the Extreme* (Chicago: Chicago Review Press, 2001), p. 182.
3. Author interview with Pat Iampietro, October 24, 2002.
4. Ibid.
5. John May, *The Greenpeace Book of Antarctica* (London: Dorling Kindersley Limited, 1989), pp. 52–53.
6. Sanford Moss, *Natural History of the Antarctic Peninsula* (New York: Columbia University Press, 1988), pp. 14–15.
7. The Wilderness Society, *Madrid Protocol on Antarctic Environmental Protection,* © 2000, <http://www.wilderness.org.au/member/tws/projects/International/madrid.html> (November 10, 2002).
8. May, p. 13.

CHAPTER 3. INTO THE FREEZING OCEAN

1. Author interview with Pat Iampietro, October 24, 2002.
2. Ibid.
3. Ibid.
4. John May, *The Greenpeace Book of Antarctica* (London: Dorling Kindersley Limited, 1989), pp. 18–19.
5. Iampietro interview.
6. May, pp. 18–19.

Chapter Notes

7. Sanford Moss, *Natural History of the Antarctic Peninsula* (New York: Columbia University Press, 1988), p. 70.

8. May, p. 82.

9. Moss, p. 79.

10. Ibid., p. 74.

11. May, pp. 82–83.

12. Ibid., pp. 98–103.

13. Ibid., p. 104.

CHAPTER 4. DESCENT TO THE BOTTOM

1. Author interview with Pat Iampietro, October 24, 2002.

2. Ibid.

3. John May, *The Greenpeace Book of Antarctica* (London: Dorling Kindersley Limited, 1989), p. 76.

4. Lynn Margulis and Karlene V. Schwartz, *Five Kingdoms: An Illustrated Guide to the Phyla of Life on Earth* (New York: W. H. Freeman and Co., 1988), p. 190.

5. Iampietro interview.

6. Ibid.

7. Ibid.

CHAPTER 5. BACK TO THE SURFACE

1. Author interview with Pat Iampietro, October 24, 2002.

2. Ibid.

3. Ibid.

auger—A large metal screw for drilling holes in dirt, rock, or ice.

baleen—Elastic strips in a whale's mouth that are used to filter krill and plankton.

blubber—A thick layer of fat on the bodies of seals and whales.

buoyancy—The ability of a submarine or a diver to go up or down in the water.

dehydration—Sickness caused by lack of water.

extinct—Vanished from the earth.

krill—Small crustaceans that live in the ocean.

magnetism—The force of attraction caused by a magnetic field.

plankton—Any living organism that cannot swim against the current of the sea. It is usually microscopic.

pollution—Harmful chemicals, oil, and debris in the ocean.

regulator—A valve that controls the flow of air from a diving tank to the diver.

scuba—*S*elf-*c*ontained *u*nderwater *b*reathing *a*pparatus. Equipment that allows divers to swim underwater to depths of about 200 feet (60 meters) using tanks of air carried on their backs.

strobe light—A bright, flashing electric light.

Further Reading

BOOKS

Burleigh, Robert. *Black Whiteness: Admiral Byrd Alone in the Antarctic.* New York: Simon & Schuster, 1998.

Conlon, Kathy. *Under the Ice.* Toronto: Kids Can Press Ltd., 2002.

Dewey, Jennifer. *Antarctic Journal: Four Months at the Bottom of the World.* New York: HarperCollins, 2001.

Loewen, Nancy, and Ann Bancroft. *Four to the Pole! The American Women's Expedition to Antarctica, 1992–93.* New York: Shoe String Press, 2001.

McGonigal, David, and Lynn Woodworth. *Antarctica and the Arctic: The Complete Encyclopedia.* New York: Firefly Books, 2001.

McMillan, Bruce. *Summer Ice: Life Along the Antarctic Peninsula.* New York: Houghton Mifflin, 1995.

Woods, Michael. *Science on Ice: Research in the Antarctic.* New York: Millbrook Press, 1995.

INTERNET ADDRESSES

Central Intelligence Agency. *The World Fact Book 2002.* "Antarctica." © 2002. <http://www.odci.gov/cia/publications/factbook/geos/ay.html>

Mastro, Jim. *National Wildlife Federation.* "Oasis Under the Ice." © 1997. <http://www.nwf.org/internationalwildlife/antarc97.html>

National Science Foundation. *Underwater Field Guide to Ross Island and McMurdo Sound, Antarctica.* © 2002. <http://scilib.ucsd.edu/sio/nsf/fguide/>

Index